Hurdle Race Marketing

Klaus Backhaus

Hurdle Race
Marketing

The Enlightenment –
The Disillusionment –
The Breakthrough

Illustrated by Karen Krings
Translated by Dianne West

 Springer Gabler

Prof. Dr. Dr. h.c. Klaus Backhaus
Muenster, Germany

ISBN 978-3-658-02443-7   ISBN 978-3-658-02444-4 (eBook)
DOI 10.1007/978-3-658-02444-4

The Deutsche Nationalbibliothek lists this publication in the Deutsche Nationalbibliografie; detailed bibliographic data are available in the Internet at http://dnb.d-nb.de.

Library of Congress Control Number: 2013956594

Springer Gabler

Editors: Barbara Roscher, Angela Pfeiffer
Cover Illustration: Karen Krings

Printed on acid-free paper

Springer Gabler is a brand of Springer DE. Springer DE is part of Springer Science+Business Media.
www.springer-gabler.de

Preface

The book "Hurdle Race Marketing" ("Hindernislauf Marketing") is aimed at practitioners, or to be more precise at all those who have already tried to align a company in keeping with the needs and conditions of the market or still intend to do so. You will doubtless rediscover a great deal that you already know from your own past experience. I was fortunate enough to find partners on the operational side who not only supported the fundamental ideas expressed in this book but also rendered financial assistance. With regard to the German text this refers specifically to the following companies to whom I express my most sincere thanks and gratitude:

GILDEMEISTER

HPP

Harnischfeger, Pietsch & Partner
Strategie- und Marketingberatung GmbH

The English version was initiated by Gildemeister, to whom I am grateful not only for the idea but also for the offer to provide an English translation of the German text. The translation was carried out by Dianne West, whom I thank most sincerely for the sensitive and insightful way in which she has handled the subject matter. It is evident from reading the translation that Dianne has managed to strike the right chord to match the tone that characterizes the German original.

Preface

The firm referred to in this book is purely fictitious, simply serving as a springboard for presenting my experience of cultural change processes spanning more than three decades. In doing so, it should be made clear that much of what is "sold" in practice under the guise of a pronounced market orientation is nothing more than a proclaimed market orientation with a missing action component. One could equally describe it as: the telling of a fairy tale. Inasmuch "Hurdle Race Marketing" revisits my previous publication „Das Märchen vom MARKETING ... aber wir sind doch alle so marktorientiert" ("The Fairy Tale of Marketing … but we are all so market-oriented") that was published in 3 editions (long since out of print) by the Schaeffer-Poeschel Verlag, Stuttgart, and continues the basic ideas of the fairy tale.

This book attempts to drive home in an amusing way what marketing really means in practice in the sense of a market-oriented management.

In doing so, however, it does have a more serious core: the point is clearly made that the internal commitment to market orientation, in other words the attitudes and practices within a company, frequently represents a bigger hurdle than the external orientation. This fact is a central feature of the three phases that any company must undergo if it is to become truly market-oriented: these are the enlightenment phase, the disillusionment phase and the breakthrough phase.

I would have been unable to write this book without the help of others. Special thanks go to my friend

Preface

and colleague, Dr. Wulff Plinke, Professor at the Humboldt University of Berlin and Founding Dean at the European School of Management and Technology (ESMT), Berlin, who assiduously studied the first drafts and assisted me time and again by improving the structure of the book as well as individual formulations, thereby helping to make it considerably more reader-friendly. It is to his credit that the book pursues a distinct "mission" that is clearly explained at the end of each section.

The responsibility for typing out the manuscript was assumed by Gabriele Rüter and Birgit Bohnenkamp, both of whom mastered the task in their usual competent manner. My sincere thanks to them also.

And last but not least, my thanks must also go to Barbara Roscher and Angela Pfeiffer from Springer Gabler who showed great commitment in driving this project forwards.

Muenster, Germany   *Klaus Backhaus*

Contents

First Part

The Enlightenment

The Enlightenment

There was once a German engineering company bearing the proud name "Deutsche Maschinenbau AG". Many knew it simply under the abbreviation DMA. Within a few short years DMA had developed into an internationally renowned brand. After many raging autumnal storms that shook the engineering industry most violently, DMA arose out of the merger of three individual companies. This merger, which for a long time was opposed by the old owners, all of whom presented themselves as die-hard patriarchs, ultimately proved extraordinarily successful.

Today the management was particularly proud of the fact that DMA had since become well known worldwide for its high-quality products. The DMA brand shone bright in vibrant red over the corporate headquarters in Bilfingen signalling: here in the provincial town Bilfingen beats the heart of internationally successful German engineering. This had not always been so.

Ernest Grey, called Ernie, a certified engineer and Chairman of the Board, was particularly proud of his company's market orientation. He used every opportunity to emphasize the image that the company had established for itself over the years. "Take, for instance, our automatic lathes" – he liked to say during trade fair presentations – "You won't find anything comparable in the entire world. We design each machine in such a way that it always meets the customer's full range of functional requirements 100 percent. We leave nothing to be desired! In the process, we make our machines so robust that downtimes are reduced to a minimum. And you know that a constant complaint of our customers' foremen is that downtimes are the bane of their working day. More market orientation isn't conceivable. On the contrary: we live for our brand. The market also takes a favourable view of the fact that we turn out at least three innovations every year. And most times it greedily sucks them up – even despite the odd flop. Year on year we show the market our technological leadership, thus demonstrating what we are capable of. And in doing so we make markets!"

What distressed Ernie Grey, however, was that despite the extremely high product quality, in the last financial year the market shares had drastically declined. During the monthly board dinner he was at pains to stress: "Our product quality is still unsurpassed". His only plausible explanation was that the sales department was obviously failing. Head of Sales, Dave Pusher, who was not only in charge of the sales offices but also responsible for sales and distribution via the trade, rejected this supposition most vehemently. "We've had the same sales people for years, so why should they now be less good at their job? Their income depends on their sales success and they are therefore highly motivated. They anticipate the customer's every wish. Sales people are a special breed." He brought his hand down on the table with such force that the glasses were in danger of toppling over. This simply served to confirm the prejudices already existing in other functional areas.

Thus in the R&D department the sales force was somewhat disrespectfully referred to as "The Boys from the Campari Front". The sales people had earned this value judgement on account of the fact that they regularly submitted the highest expenses claims. There was therefore a widespread view throughout DMA that selling took place first and foremost during joint lunches or on the golf course.

This image of the sales force was, however, equally encouraged by the sales people themselves. With a reputation for playing to the gallery, the people from Sales were never short of a gag. Every employee in the company, irrespective of the department, had some tale of Sales to tell. Statements made by sales people such as "How should I know what I'm thinking before I can hear what I'm saying?" or "If I were you, I'd want to be me again" – a quote from a cartoon – had done the rounds and in the eyes of many throughout the company were proof of the platitudes on the sales scene.

On the other hand everyone was aware that without Sales they wouldn't be better off either because then there would be no revenue. Thus at every event sales boss Dave Pusher never grew tired of emphasizing that the cost-cutting measures implemented time and again by the management made little sense when applied as a stand-alone strategy. He was accustomed to saying: "If we just want to minimize costs, then we should close up shop. We can't imagine a better cost situation!" At least with this remark he usually got everyone to laugh with him. He was then inclined to put more wood on the fire, often continuing as if giving a lecture: "It's solely the difference between revenue and costs which should be as big as possible. With this goal in mind, cost-cutting makes sense. But the revenue side of things also plays a part – and that's where Sales comes in. My boys know that. But we can't do anything if the prices aren't right and these are largely determined by Production. The prices we get quoted from here are mostly utopian. As a result, we frequently calculate ourselves out of the market."

These hypotheses, which Dave Pusher had put forward during one of the last board meetings, brought Plant Manager, Henry Workman, a graduate engineer who had been suffering from high blood pressure for years, almost to boiling point: "Gentlemen, that just won't do", he grumbled during the course of the formal dinner. "Quality has its price. I've squeezed the very last rationalization margins out of production. If we were to produce greater quantities, we could exploit the experience curve effects associated with higher volumes. But Sales is asleep here. As you know, we have chosen to pursue indirect selling via the trade. The problem with this is that dealers have their own interests to protect and sell a broad range of different brands. They are therefore less interested in selling one specific product. The machine dealer is essentially a box mover who is interested above all in quantity. It is of little interest to him with which brand he achieves it. That's why we need our own sales organization. And that's why we should increasingly favour direct sales."

The Enlightenment

The plant manager, who had just finished spooning up his soup, ranked at DMA as a longstanding experienced member of the management and was known for defending his interests with great skill. Dave Pusher was aware that if it came to a clash of opinions with Henry Workman he would more than likely draw the short straw. This applied to the price calculation issue in particular. It was almost a tradition at DMA that Sales had only a rough idea of the costs that were actually incurred. This was due to the fact that the management pursued a strategy of decentralizing pricing decisions, in other words of leaving it mainly to the individual sales staff to decide what prices should ultimately be charged. At the same time, however, the sales staff had only been given general information about the total costs, so that in cost terms the price floor could not be so easily determined. At a further training congress Henry Workman had learned that in negotiations costs act as a price pressure brake, along the lines: the greater the costs allocated to an order, the higher the final negotiated price will be. Henry Workman, who as an engineer was particularly open to rational arguments, remarked somewhat derisively: "You have to approach sales people from a psychological angle. They're all psychopaths controlled by customers like marionettes."

Despite harbouring certain prejudices, Henry Workman nevertheless believed that the sales force needed supporting: "What's called for is a computer-aided CRM system that allows our sales people to work increasingly with more objective figures." Dave Pusher, always sceptical whenever the plant manager said anything, asked: "What is a CRM system anyway? More than likely another IT-driven system, used by Sales to endlessly query and evaluate our knowledge before allowing it to disappear into some database or other. I tell you, our business is in our heads, we don't need any IT. It's all a senseless additional burden for my people. They need to analyze the white in the eyes of the customers and sell, sell, sell ... With a CRM system we would simply be throwing money out of the window!"

In response to this Head of Finance, Dodo von Goldberg, took to the floor: "IT investments require special scrutiny by the finance department. As you know, gentlemen, the post calculations of our IT investments have shown that none, and I emphasize none of our IT investments in the past have been cost-effective or yielded any real return. We are losing a great deal of money here. Moreover, most of these investments affect profits right from the outset because large parts of them cannot be activated. It seems to me that investing in an optimized production would make more sense."

Optimized production was the buzzword for the Plant Manager, Henry Workman, who responded to it immediately: "Sales people sell investments like 'CRM' as 'market investments'. That's all a load of nonsense. These aren't investments at all. Investments are, after all, things like new production lines or new system headquarters. Put simply, investments are something you can inaugurate with a barbecue and a brass band, once you can see how expenditure has materialized."

"No", the R&D Manager, Dr. Tinkering, interjected, "we have already heard that production is largely optimized. We need to further develop our product quality. Standing still means taking a step backwards. We must re-invest more money in development, also with regard to machinery. Where funds flow to cannot be decided based solely on accounting considerations. If we allow our bookkeepers to decide how we develop our future technology, then we can say goodbye to DMA." The development manager's words were greeted with applause.

Sitting on the fringe, Head of Marketing, Mr. Etting, who was usually addressed in the company by his first name only, which was Mark, had been trying to get a word in for quite some time. "I've been preaching for years that we need a stronger market orientation. Our people think only in terms of products and not in terms of markets. I would like once more to ..."

Managing Director Ernie Grey cut him short: "I think that will do for now. In our line of business we won't sell anything with advertising and brochures. Next year we'll have to reduce our general marketing costs by 20 percent anyway."

The general nodding of heads confirmed that in this point at least the participants were obviously of one accord. "Nevertheless, gentlemen" he went on to say "we can't carry on like this. Every single one of us has his own idea about how in our business sector, machine tools, we can win back our lost market shares. But what we need is a common market-oriented strategy. This is also the concern of our supervisory board."

Chairwoman of the Supervisory Board, Dr. Stella Steel, who had the reputation of serving the company not so much as a good fairy but rather as a taskmistress demanding hard-hitting results, had assured her support in developing measures for a common successful market strategy. This was all the more remarkable since within the company Stella Steel would not normally be seen as marketing-minded. "We should use this unique opportunity", Ernie Grey called out to his managerial colleagues who, however, were busy with their dessert, a crème brûlée and a white mousse au chocolat, along and with praising the excellent sweet Sauternes that accompanied it.

The next few weeks passed with all the participants working on measures to achieve a stronger market orientation. The number of suggestions that had come together after four weeks was impressive. The only problem was that they covered many points that had been discussed time and again before: a new CRM system, price reductions, sales optimization, optimization of production and a long list of other suggestions. This being the case, Ernie Grey was not at all satisfied with the result. "Too conventional and not creative enough" was his comment. Without any long discussion, the decision was therefore made to call in the consulting firm McArthur Company (MAC) from Boston.

MAC scrutinized the company for two long months, followed by a concluding presentation on DMA premises. The recommendations led to some gripping politics: an overheads value analysis had shown that up to 40 percent of overheads could be saved. Using a sound business sector portfolio it was possible to clearly show that the business sector "Lathe Machines" was among the so called stars.

Dr. Stuart Smart, a MAC partner, therefore consistently emphasized in a most convincing way: "Mistakes have been made with lathe machines because you don't lose market shares with stars."

This conclusion impressed the management profoundly. Although neither new nor a surprise, never before had anyone heard such a soundly reasoned justification.

It took a few days before all the participants had acquainted themselves in detail with the recommendations of the consultants. The first person to resume the discussion was the Chief Financial Officer, the business studies graduate Mike Controllieri. "Gentlemen", he announced at a management meeting, "the latest figures show that our business sector 'Lathe Machines' continues to spiral downwards. In the last month alone we have suffered a 10 percent loss in turnover – and that at a time when the economy is booming. What can we then expect if the economy should deteriorate?"

Mark Etting, the person most affected by the measures to reduce overheads got to his feet to make a brief presentation: "Gentlemen, I know that a lot of you here today would prefer to do away with my department altogether because in the eyes of many Marketing would then for the first time make a measurable contribution towards earnings. But that simply shows me how self-obsessed we always seem to be. If I review our entire discussion so far, then the word 'customer' has been used quite frequently. Even so, I maintain that we are failing to understand our customers properly. As part of our market research, I have used the time since our last discussion to obtain information explaining what the customer thinks of our machines. And I believe I have some indicators as to why we are constantly suffering losses in both market shares and turnover in connection with our machines." The remaining gentlemen of the management had in the meantime pricked up their ears and suddenly showed great interest, manifesting itself in a tense silence.

"As our Head of Sales, Dave Pusher, has confirmed, the tradition has always been for our sales people to visit the customers' plant managers, with whom they have established excellent personal relations", Mark Etting went on to explain, "plant managers think in terms of downtime and flexibility in order to be able to solve any problems arising with the respective machine. In this respect our machines are certainly the best. But that's just one side of the coin. Our customers are also under increasing cost pressure. Our Chinese counterparts, whom we have been quick to mock in the past, have redefined the rules of the market. They offer significantly lower-performance machines but bring the cost-effectiveness argument into play. Their strategy is to try and sell their cheaper, low-end standard machines, which offer at the most 80 percent of the functions of our machines, by bringing them to the market through another channel, the so called Buying Center."

"We cannot and don't want to compare our products with the Chinese machines", Dave Pusher interrupted.

"That's the whole point", Mark Etting went on to say, "perhaps we don't but our customers certainly do. Whether we want to or not doesn't matter. Whether we succeed or fail in the market is decided solely by the customer. And the worrying thing is that we're suffering our greatest loss in turnover among our biggest customers, each of whom uses at least several of our machines. And I can also tell you why: the last 20 percent of the functions offered by our machines are only rarely needed by the customer. If the customer buys five machines of the same type, buying one from us and the other four as cheaper standard Chinese machines, then overall he has 100 percent functional fulfilment – but at a much more cost-effective price! The customer simply buys from the supplier who in his subjective view comes up with the best offer – in other words the one having a Comparative Competitive Advantage, in short a CCA!"

The gentlemen of the management looked defeatedly at the floor. Once again Ernie Grey was the first to speak: "Mark, I don't think I've ever experienced you quite like this before! You really have got to the crux of our problem. What precisely is this CCA? Isn't it the same as a Unique Selling Proposition, in short USP?" Mark replied that he would be happy to explain this to them. "For me", he went on to say, "the CCA is the navigator that guides me through the rough seas of volatile markets. Provided we don't lose sight of our CCA, there's not a lot that can happen to us", Mark Etting, getting slightly hot under the collar, went on to say.

"I have a request", Ernie Grey interrupted, "this CCA seems to be so important that we should give Mark Etting the chance to prepare this part thoroughly. I propose that we get together again in 14 days time for a special CCA meeting." The proposal found general approval and a date was set for a meeting two weeks later.

Mark Etting used these two weeks to prepare himself intensively for what he considered to be the most important presentation of his life. He knew he wouldn't get a second chance. He wanted to use his presentation to shed new light on his role in the company. To this end he would ask the Chairman of the Management Board to fulfil three wishes. This would be the "cherry on top". And he was sure that it would help him to reach an unexpected highpoint in his presentation. Insofar, his three wishes were to be a real surprise. Due to the importance of the subject-matter, a time-frame of 2 hours had been allocated. Mark Etting knew that it was essential for him to stick to this time.

It would be even better still if he were able to finish a little earlier and thus create time for an in-depth discussion, which he had high hopes for.

On the morning of the CCA meeting Mark Etting was somewhat nervous. He put on his best suit and set off in good time to give himself the chance of checking whether the technical equipment needed for his presentation was indeed working properly. He needn't have worried – the technicians had done their job properly. Thus, the meeting kicked off promptly at 9 a.m.

Mark began his presentation in a professorial tone. "What is marketing?" was the stand-alone sentence on his first film. He knew that the members of the management would immediately fall back on their old understanding of marketing, identifying it with advertising. He wanted to confront this right from the word go – even at the cost of sounding professor-like. However, he hoped to counteract this professor image by inserting a prologue ahead of his actual presentation: "Gentlemen, as you know, I am a native of Muenster (Germany). In the Muenster region hot-air ballooning is a popular pastime. In the lead-up to my presentation I would like to tell you the story of two balloonists from Muenster.

One day two balloonists from Muenster climb into a hot-air balloon. The weather is perfect. They soar up high over green meadows and hedge banks. After thirty minutes they come up against a thick wall of clouds, causing them to lose all orientation. After another 30 minutes the cloud cover breaks up. Down below they see a man on his own, leaning against a fence. They reduce their altitude slightly to come within calling distance. 'Where are we?' one of the balloonists calls out. The man leaning on the fence calls back: 'In a balloon.' Thereupon the one balloonist says to the other: 'We're still in the Muenster region. That man down there is obviously a professor of marketing.' 'Why?' the other asks. 'His statement was accurate but lacking in content.' Gentlemen, this is something I'd like to protect you from. But there's little danger of that in my case. After all, I'm not a professor." A single laugh was quickly followed by an entire peal of laughter.

After having "loosened up" the atmosphere a little in this way, he knew that he must quickly be serious again. That's why his next film showed his definition of marketing: **Marketing is the Management of CCAs.** By this time Mark had slowly warmed up and his presentation increasingly lost its initial professorial tone. "Contrary to the opinion of many in the company marketing is

– not identical with advertising,

– nor is it the English term for sales,

– nor is it a suitable tool for getting customers to make purchases they really don't want to make.

Gentlemen, it is necessary to understand that marketing has nothing to do with dubious things. On the contrary: in the definition of marketing as the management of CCAs it becomes clear that marketing is a fundamental management function.

On the other hand, marketing does not mean fulfilling the customer's every wish either, but only those wishes which are likely to lead to profit. This, of course, presupposes that in the eyes of customers you are able to distinguish yourself from your competitors. Being better than your competitors at fulfilling customers' wishes means being effective. But from the supplier's perspective it must also be clear that effectiveness as the sole consideration is too restrictive. It must be complemented by an efficiency analysis. That's why it is not the objective of marketing to fulfil customers' wishes but rather to achieve profits. The way to accomplish this lies in satisfying customers' needs. But – if you'll allow me to point out, Mr. Grey –, fulfilling customers' wishes 100 percent, as you maintained at the beginning, is not our objective. It's sufficient to satisfy 80 percent of the customers' wishes if the relevant competitors can only satisfy 70 percent of them. Thus we must be better than our competitors in our perception of consumers and – that's incredibly important – because it must pay off for us as well. This balancing act between effectiveness (satisfying the customer) and efficiency (doing it cost-effectively) is the challenge of market orientation. Bearing this in mind, it is then also clear that the CCA is not the same as the

USP. The USP is something that describes our service and product portfolio compared with the competition. Crudely put: 'Do we have anything in the customers' perception world that distinguishes our offer from that of our competitors?' This distinguishing feature is the USP, the uniqueness of our offering. The CCA also encompasses these perspectives, but enhances them by virtue of a customer and an efficiency consideration which compares the price and costs of the service offering."

Both plant manager and head of R&D had listened intently. "Mark, you emphasize time and again that in the customers' perception world we have to hold a specific position. But we sell technically-oriented products, namely machines. These machines have an objectively ascertainable performance capability and that's why in our understanding the emphasis on the customers' perception world is the wrong approach." "Here we differ quite significantly", Mark Etting responded. "For us as marketing people only the customers' subjective world is what counts. Since the purchasing behaviour of customers is directly linked to how they perceive the offer. This potentially distorted perception world controls their behaviour."

Because Mark Etting already knew this argument, he had brought with him a photo that would make it clear that perception can lead to a completely different judgement than the one that the objective facts actually reveal. To get this across, he presented an advertisement opposing the use of cocaine. You'll find this advertisement on the next page of the book. Were you to judge this young man, you would perhaps come to the conclusion that he is not such a bad type. On now turning the book around 180 degrees, you then see that this friendly demeanour is perceived differently depending on the angle from which the photo is viewed."

Mark Etting had prepared this to prove his point, just in case one of the engineers expressed doubt that subjective perception could be a behaviour-controlling element.

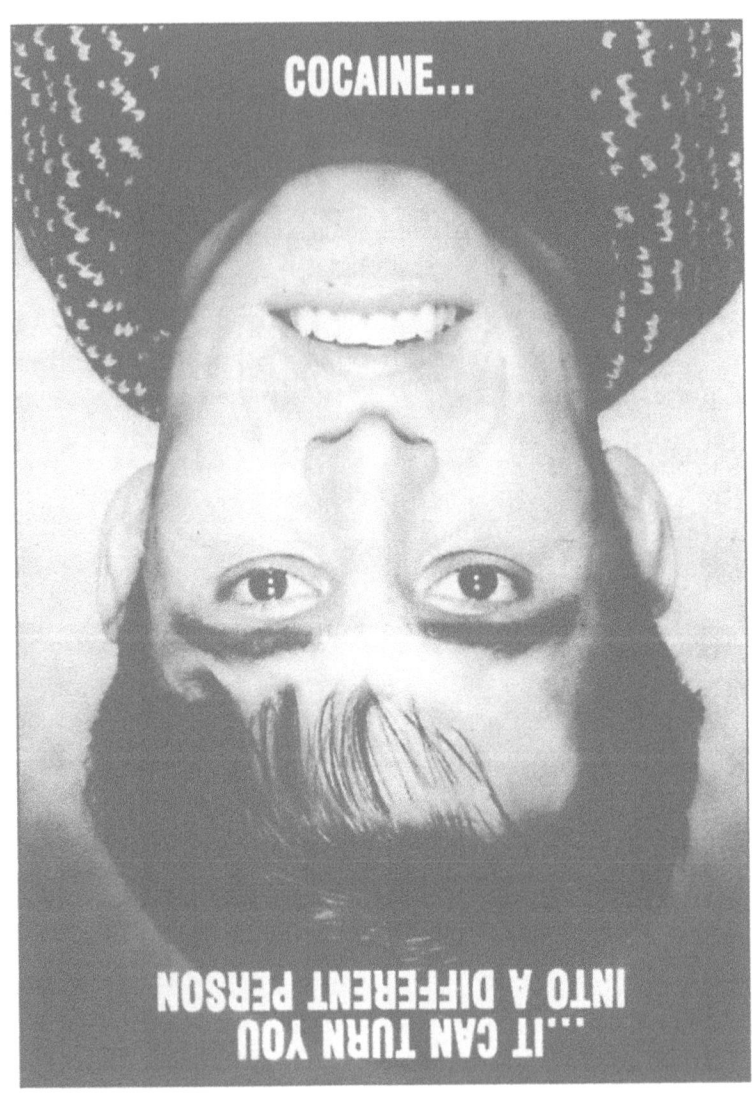

Source: Robin Landa, Graphic Design Solutions,
4th ed., Wadsworth Publishing 2012, S. 282

This time the example hit home. Both Dr. Tinkering as well as Henry Workman had run out of arguments. Mark Etting therefore proceeded to slowly bring his presentation to a conclusion. Turning to Ernie Grey he said: "Mr. Grey you may not be a fairy godmother with the capacity to fulfil every wish but I would nevertheless like to ask you to allow me to express three wishes." "Granted", Ernie Grey replied, having become more jovial in the meantime, "even though I don't yet know what these wishes will be."

"My first wish is that each member of the management present today should write down for their area what contribution it makes towards the CCA. My second wish is that we do the same with all the staff working in a value chain – from R&D to Purchasing and from Production to Sales – by asking them to write down, obscured from others, where they believe their own CCA lies. And thirdly – and in saying this Mark Etting produced a slight smile – I would like to ask you to close the marketing department down in order to demonstrate our market orientation also to the outside world."

The entire management was stunned. There was soon unanimity that the first two wishes could and should be fulfilled as quickly as possible. But there was some perplexity over the request to abolish the marketing department altogether. Henry Workman was the first to regain his composure. "I don't understand it Mr. Etting. For the first time we are about to get all enthusiastic about marketing because you have taught us that marketing is more than simply painting colourful pictures and distributing brochures. For me this is a kind of epiphany: Then you go on to propose that the marketing department be abolished. That's totally inconsistent!" "On the contrary, Mr. Workman", Mark Etting responded. "The way in which the marketing department is organized in our company spells death for a company's market orientation and for marketing with it. Actually, we won't need a marketing department again until the market orientation idea is firmly anchored in the attitudes and practices of the company's employees. It will then become apparent that there is a range of coordination tasks for which a department must then be responsible. The way our marketing department has now been organized means that it is rightly understood as nothing more than a generator of overheads. But that is inappropriate and unreasonable. Marketing is much more. It is a way of thinking, an attitude – or as the Americans like to say – it is a shared value for everyone involved. A traditional marketing department simply diverts attention away from what marketing really wants: to generate a sustained increase in revenue and earnings. This is rather a task for everyone in the company. It cannot be delegated to a marketing department – as a small box in our company's organizational chart. That's why – for the time being at least – I would like our marketing department to be closed down.

The five employees of my department will go out into the ranks as ambassadors and drive the CCA idea forward. In order to do this, my first two wishes must be fulfilled. I would like to show that none of you now present and working in a value chain, the management included, has a uniform understanding of what their CCA is or should be. If this is so, then we must first work at finding a common CCA understanding within a value chain. It is precisely here where we must start and this is where for me the task of the five members of my former marketing department lies: to implement this in the front line."

Mark Etting's presentation had taken the management by storm. A new mood of invigoration became palpable. "Let us implement these ideas as quickly as possible", Dr. Tinkering called out into the room. "My developers must also learn to think early on in terms of market ideas." Suddenly everyone started to talk at the same time. A jolt had gone through the company and Mark Etting wanted to take full advantage of it.

What has happened here? For the first time the responsible office-holders have recognized that marketing

- is not an organizational unit that focuses exclusively in the company on marketing;

- demands cross-functional practices;

- represents an executive function in the top management which cannot be delegated;

- concerns all the employees of an organization.

They had quite literally seen the light – they realize that the CCA stands for a common principle, a compass that applies to all functions, that they can use to orientate themselves by and that can show everyone simultaneously the way to success in a competitive world.

This enlightenment can mobilize a major force because the functional and departmental egotism suddenly seems less of an obstacle, but rather a common understanding shared by all appears to be truly achievable. That this state of enlightenment could be reached is largely due to the crisis sensed by all. In such situations it is clear to everyone that something must happen.

Let's take a look at what Mark and his colleagues do in order to allow this force to be effective for DMA.

Second Part
The Disillusionment

The Disillusionment

Mark Etting wanted as quickly as possible to take advantage of the current favourable situation and the new mood of invigoration to set the pending processes of change in motion. „The soup must be eaten while still hot", he thought, knowing full well that the original saying actually goes somewhat differently. As early as the week following he therefore circulated an e-mail among all members of the management asking them to fulfil his first two wishes. Everything went smoothly.

The members of the management team came with their most important staff in order to take part in the CCA experiment.

For this purpose Mark Etting had reserved DMA's largest lecture hall for half a day. He opened the session in the morning with an impassioned speech in which he once again explained to the participants what a CCA is. "The CCA has an effectiveness and an efficiency dimension" he began. "As regards the effectiveness dimension we must consider which of our customers' wishes we want to fulfil and how we can succeed against our competitors. But at the same time the efficiency problem has also be taken into account, by fulfilling in the final analysis only those wishes which can be expected to generate a positive contribution to our profitability. Only those companies which are not only successful against the competition but also manage to turn this acceptance success into economic success, can be said to have a CCA.

Ladies and gentlemen, you have already seated yourselves such that the right members are already sitting together. I would like to ask the individual members of a value chain to please define what their CCA is. Each member working in isolation should note on a prepared sheet what this CCA position is. I will then collect in the sheets."

Peter Roleman, a member of staff from Mark Etting's department, and who everyone in the company called PR, handed out to each participant white sheets of paper which they would be able to use to note down their own perceived CCA. A general air of hustle and bustle spread throughout the room. Some tried to whisper among themselves, which didn't escape Mark Etting's attention. "Ladies and Gentlemen, please define your CCA without communicating with your colleagues. Coordinated or collusive behaviour – as in real life – is not permitted." Most of the workshop participants chuckled quietly to themselves.

After roughly 30 minutes all the participants appeared to have completed the task. While Mark collected together all the filled out sheets, a quiet discussion ensued that didn't even subside during the coffee-break provided at the end. "What did you define as our CCA?", Birgit B. Blue, who everyone simply called "Triple B", asked her boss, Head of Purchasing, Dick Discount. For him it was fairly clear: "It's the favourable purchase prices negotiated by myself and my team which create a price advantage for us at the sales end." Triple B, who was a member of Dave Pusher's sales team, immediately called these facts into question. "To think that we should have a price CCA thanks to you is simply ridiculous! We may indeed have reduced our costs slightly, but that in no way goes far enough to allow us to compete against the Japanese and above all in future against the Chinese.

It's not a matter of our having made every endeavour to reduce our costs. We need to reduce them to such an extent that in the eyes of the consumers we offer a price advantage. That's our real task – and only then will we have the basis for a CCA."

"What have you then defined as our CCA?", Dick Discount asked Triple B. "I believe that our CCA lies in our quick delivery time. Thanks to our location benefits we are already quicker in responding to German customers than the Chinese", Triple B was keen to stress. "But that's sheer nonsense", Dick Discount replied. "You sales people have only an eye for the Japanese and more recently also for the Chinese and Indians. But I tell you, our German competitors, especially the company Heidenreich, offer even shorter delivery times than we have", Dick Discount interjected.

"Perhaps we don't have a CCA at all" Triple B sighed and in doing so looked at Dick Discount with an air of uncertainty. "We'll find out after the coffee-break" she told Dick Discount and then proceeded to drink her latte macchiato which had gone almost completely cold in the meantime.

Although conversations were in progress and were being conducted more intensively than ever before, Mark Etting clapped his hands saying: "Ladies and gentlemen, may I ask you to rejoin the plenary session?" The participants returned, albeit somewhat slowly, to the lecture hall. Mark Etting had used the time during the break to quickly study the CCA sheets and give the answers a specific structure.

"Ladies and gentlemen, you won't believe it, but it's true: the fulfilment of my first two wishes has produced precisely the result I had expected. Here in this workshop four value chains are represented, in other words four divisions all selling machines, but with different technologies in different markets. Each value chain respectively is responsible for achieving their prescribed targets.

But our targets are not quality-related but exclusively geared to quantity. We plan turnover, we plan earnings, we plan order intake. What we do not plan is our CCA position. Here everything gets muddled up. I would like to cite the example of value chain 3. This value chain is represented by four members of staff besides the managing director in charge. Birgit B. Blue from Sales, Christian Brown from Production, Dick Discount from Purchasing and Hubert Fox from R&D. Without wanting to assign the answers to any individuals, we have in the case of five persons across all the value chains eight different definitions of what characterizes the CCA position of this division in the market. I would like to read out the CCA positions to you.

(1) We are the cheapest.

(2) We have the best delivery times.

(3) Our CCA is our quality.

(4) We are problem-solvers.

(5) We are the only ones with a performance-graduated, continuous automation system with optional solution components for all application purposes..

(6) We are the biggest player in the global market.

(7) We are the technological leader.

(8) For us the customer is king.

I would now like to ask all those present: What do you think of these CCAs?"

On hearing the list of CCAs from value chain 3 the other participants started to grin. "Just wait", Mark Etting thought to himself. "Your turn will come!"

In order to objectify and not personalize the entire discussion, as well as assign the matter as a whole to individual value chains, I propose – and thank you already for agreeing to it – that we take a closer look at the eight CCAs formulated. „What do you think of CCA number 1:

(1) We are the cheapest."

Without hesitating, Dick Discount immediately took the floor. „Although Mark Etting has assured us that the individual CCAs will not be personalized, I would nevertheless like to come out into the open here. As head of purchasing I feel entitled to maintain that thanks to the excellent work of the purchasing de-

partment we make a key contribution to our favourable costs situation and thus create the basis for a price
CCA." Birgit B. Blue, whom everyone knew belonged
to the same value chain and occasionally liked to get
into a spat with Dick Discount, although the two were
on first-name terms, responded thus: "My dear Dick,
nobody here doubts for one minute that you don't
have your purchasing department under control. But
Purchasing only accounts for roughly ten percent of
the overall costs of our machines. If Production doesn't
operate ,cleanly', then the advantage you've achieved
on the purchasing side is quickly forfeited along the
value chain." Christian Brown, Head of Production in
the value chain concerned, could hardly believe his
ears: „You, Mrs. Blue, thus maintain that in our sup-
plementary calculation we gamble away the advantages that Dick Discount has managed to gain for
us! I must refute these assertions most vigorously. Our
internal transfer pricing system clearly shows that we
are indeed responsible for the largest portion of the
costs of a machine. But we have demonstrated that
over the past few years we have been in a position to
refrain from enforcing price increases." "That wasn't
the point I was making at all", Birgit B. Blue responded, "I simply wanted to point out that no matter how
hard Dick may try, his influence over our price CCA
situation is nevertheless limited. I know that Dick is
the born buyer. You will know that born buyers are
characterized by the fact that the first word they express as babies isn't 'mummy' or 'daddy' – as is nor-

mally the case – but rather 'discount'. I'm sure that if Dick's parents were still alive, they would confirm this."

Somehow a spanner had got in the works of value chain 3. The short discussion had shown that there still wasn't any coherent understanding of what one could term a common CCA strategy. They were all pulling together but were not aware that this was simply a necessary requirement for good collaboration. It is, after all, crucial to also pull in the same direction.

Mark Etting took the floor: "We don't want to get personal here. But this discussion shows me that my hypothesis was obviously correct. Despite all the euphoria there's still a lot of discussing to be done before per value chain a CCA position can be defined that is acceptable to everyone. Let us further discuss the other CCAs without getting too emotional about it – although I do consider empathy to be a desirable trait. I propose that we now move on to the next perceived CCA position:

(2) Wir haben die besten Lieferzeiten.

Would anyone in the room care to comment on this?" Simon Preston, a member of the sales staff from value chain 4, interjected that this was a question of the facts. „If a value chain has indeed the best delivery times compared with all the other competitors, then this can constitute a CCA – at least as far as the effectiveness side of things is concerned." Birgit B. Blue, who in the meantime had clearly talked herself warm, intercepted:

"If the customer isn't at all interested in reduced delivery times, then the best delivery time in the world is worthless! I can cite examples where shorter delivery times can create real difficulties for a customer. If you deliver at short notice, the customer has to create expensive warehouse capacities. And he just doesn't have the facilities to do that. In a case like this the advantage does not meet the criterion (significance)."

Mark Etting was thrilled: „It would seem that we are now leaving the confusing paths of the past and setting our sights on the clear structures of the future. Mrs. Blue, you share my sentiments entirely. Not what we can do well, and perhaps even do the best should be our guiding principle but that what the consumer needs. You have worked that out most wonderfully. Let's now focus our attention on the third CCA formulated:

(3) Our CCA is our quality.

What do you say to this CCA?" Birgit B. Blue called out to those in the room: "Where is the comparative here? Quality is everything and nothing. It's a small fig-leaf – in fact one is even tempted to call it a big fig-leaf –, that this CCA tries to cover itself up with. In order for the whole thing to become operational, we need to define what quality features we regard as affording us a CCA position. That depends among other things also on the target group. Let me demonstrate this to you by means of an example from daily life: for a business man the quality of a suit is perhaps characterized by its crease-resistance, for a doorman on the Reeperbahn, the red light district of Hamburg, perhaps more by its tear-resistance." Mark Etting, who was increasingly getting the impression that in Birgit B. Blue he had found a congenial partner, added: "Here indeed any comparative in the formulation is missing! And besides the formulation is so weak that it could cover just about anything. Here greater specificity is called for because while the price CCA is one-dimensional, a potential quality advantage can be multi-dimensional. This means that several competitors in the same market can hold market leader positions on the basis of different quality dimensions. That's why it's important not to allow it to lapse into platitudes." The term platitude threatened to evoke a confrontation. Several participants at the same time opposed such discriminating statements. „Whoever generates more platitudes here, Production or Marketing, is at this point irrelevant", one participant remarked.

It was fairly obvious that the situation was in danger of breaking down. Dr. Tinkering, Head of R&D, who was otherwise generally more pensive and in management meetings somewhat absent-minded, suddenly developed a feel for the situation. "Mrs. Blue, gentlemen, at this moment in time it's not a matter of personal issues. Mr. Etting had even proposed discussing the entire CCAs without any reference to individuals and thus without any reference to the value chain. May I remind you that we were the ones who made the whole thing personal. That's why I would not find it fair if we were to let the good ideas that Mr. Etting has provided us with over the last few sessions simply fall by the wayside. And that on account of personal sensitivities. I therefore propose that we continue discussing the potential CCAs – but I believe we should do this without getting personal. Outings are therefore out", and he delighted in the fact that he had been able to use the word "out" twice in the one sentence.

Mark Etting was secretly most thankful to Dr. Tinkering and pleased that an appointed managing director had spoken up on his behalf. He therefore took up the proposal of Dr. Tinkering immediately and moved on to the next CCA:

(4) We are problem-solvers.

Mark Etting knew that the formulation of this CCA had the potential to be a ticking time-bomb. Thereupon Triple B, Birgit B. Blue, blurted out: „I think I'll die laughing. Like CCA number 3 we again have something that doesn't look like a comparative. So, put it in the same box as potential CCA number 3 and forget about it." Birgit B. Blue was threatening slowly but surely to derail the entire workshop. That's why Mark Etting ignored this objection and tried to bring a little calm to the discussion by saying: „Sometimes it's good to ask oneself how the formulation would read the other way around. In the case of the statement 'We are problem-solvers', this would be, 'We are problem-creators.' Can you imagine that a company would want to assert this? With it we also have an answer to the question that customers now and then ask: 'Are you here to solve the problem or are you part of the problem?'"

Although no-one laughed, Mark Etting had the feeling that he had succeeded in covering up Birgit B. Blue's ill-considered comments. After this turn of events, he would have preferred to have now been at the end of the list of the CCAs. But he was only halfway through and had another four to go. „Hopefully, it'll go OK", he thought to himself, and proceeded to CCA number 5.

(5) We are the only ones having a performance-graduated, continuous automation system with optional solution components for all application purposes.

No sooner had he read it out, then a number of participants started laughing. John Runner, a sales engineer, then blurted out: "You have to attend a 14-day language course to be able to understand what's meant here." Also Triple B, Birgit B. Blue, was unable to suppress making a remark. "This CCA must have been formulated by one of our engineers: for the expert certain to be recognized as a clear advantage, but for a normal person missing the mark entirely!" "But our partners are mechatronics engineers and they know what is meant", responded Manni Meyer, a sales engineer on Dave Pusher's team.

"And they are our customers' decision-makers. Just because you don't understand it, doesn't mean that the formulation is nonsensical. You shouldn't always judge others by your own limited capabilities."

Now the attacks were starting to get personal. Mark Etting couldn't and wouldn't let that happen. "Mr. Meyer and Mrs. Blue, do you always deal with each other in this way? You both come from Dave Pusher's department! A strange departmental culture indeed! You should be careful how you talk to people. We have not come here to have you run us down. We wanted to improve and intensify our collaboration. That doesn't leave any room for personal reproaches. Ultimately, we are all sitting in the same boat. And to delight in the fact that a hole on the backboard side means that you're safe because you're sitting on the starboard side seems to me to be less than clever. If nobody finds a way to seal the hole, we'll all go down with the boat – whether we're sitting on the backboard or starboard side."

The gentlemen of the management in attendance were impressed by the way in which young Etting had summed up the matter in a nutshell and was able to diffuse an impending conflict. At one time the marketing department had gained an image that Dr. Tinkering had characterized with the slogan "Youth researches", because the six people working in the marketing department were all exceptionally young. He now wanted to correct this impression. In the meantime Mark Etting had regained the focus of the discussion and made it clear to the participants that it was impossible to tell simply from looking at the formulation of CCA number 5 whether or not it really described the effectiveness side of a CCA. He had coined the phrase "the answer to every question relating to marketing is: 'It depends …!'" "You must then be prepared for the follow-up question, which is always 'on what?'. But at least it gives you a little time to think about it some more. And that's why I'm asking you: 'How can we know whether the formulation of CCA number 5 is really reliable or not? What does it depend on?" "Triple B" and Manni Meyer, who had since come closer together again, both remarked: "On the purchase decision-makers!" "If these are the engineers of the customers, then the formulation of CCA number 5 has CCA potential", Triple B finally agreed. "And if it's Commercial Purchasing, then the formulation should be reconsidered", Mr. Meyer added. Mark Etting knew that he had taken a considerable step forward in achieving his objective of freeing marketing from its absolute position and making it a task for everyone right across the board. All he had to do now was to prevent the last three CCAs from causing the entire meeting to run up against a brickwall. He therefore immediately called:

(6) Biggest player in the global market.

While still reading the text out loud, he saw how the Chairman, Ernie Grey, was desperately turning the pages of his notebook as if searching for something important. Actually, Ernie Grey had noted down the market shares of the relevant competitors. "Apart from the fact that I doubt whether we do in fact lead the market – we sometimes tend to deceive ourselves in this respect –, at this point I would like to make it clear that the leadership position on the global market isn't a CCA but the outcome of our CCA position. Only if we were to sell by price, could the leadership position on the global market represent a potential CCA position because as the worldwide market leader we would then have to have the strongest position on the experience curve."

Mark Etting secretly congratulated himself on having plainly achieved something in the mind of his management. Dr. Tinkering, who – as always – cast a critical eye over the entire events, permitted himself to ask why in the first case the leadership position on the global market was the outcome of a CCA position, whereas in the case of a course of action based on pricing policy the leadership position on the global market could produce a CCA. Mark Etting intervened: "Dr. Tinkering, the experience curve describes a mechanism based on the assumption that with each doubling of the cumulative quantities the out of pocket costs per unit sink by 20 to 30 percent. If you are the market leader, you thus have the best cost position and can use this for creating a price leadership." Dr. Tinkering, who as a natural scientist was used to thinking in quantitative parameters, doubted this statement. "If I've understood the entire concept of the experience curve correctly, then what it boils down to is cumulative quantities. It is, however, the case that the market leader must not necessarily have the largest cumulative quantity. There can be other companies that have been on the market for much longer and therefore in the past have accumulated larger cumulative quantities." The effect this objection had on Mark Etting was immediate. It was an argument he had not at all considered. He had always quietly assumed that these effects that had been discovered in rapidly growing markets, in which the companies had entered the market at comparable times, could be readily generalized. Although Dr. Tinkering did not broach the subject again, it had become clear to Mark Etting that he had again lost ground. He realized that from now on he would have to take care not to make any further mistakes. Otherwise he feared that all the plus points he had previously gained for implementing a new understanding of marketing in the company could again be at risk. What had made him nervous above all was that Dr. Tinkering had not made any attempt to follow the matter up. Was this a sign that he had yet again abandoned any idea of a market-oriented corporate management?

"I believe that the last two CCAs you have defined can be dealt with together.

(7) 'We are the technological leader'

and

(8) 'For us the customer is king'.

I propose tackling these two points together because they are diametrically opposed. 'We are the technological leader' has initially nothing to do with the market and 'for us the customer is king' has initially nothing to do with technological leadership", was how Mark Etting kicked off the last round of discussions concerning CCAs. Mr. Fox from R&D took the floor: „These are two things which, as you have rightly pointed out, Mr. Etting, are incompatible. This is valid on account of the fact that CCA number 8 is a sentence devoid of content. What does it mean, 'for us the customer is king'?

That's a load of nonsense. It goes without saying that we treat our customers like royalty. I would like to remind you of the introductory words of our Chairman, Ernie Grey, who said some weeks ago: 'We design each machine in such a way that it always meets the customer's full range of functional requirements 100 percent. We leave nothing to be desired! More market orientation simply isn't conceivable.' But as you know, our sales have declined nonetheless. So that cannot be the stumbling block. It would therefore be better for us to distance ourselves from such clichés.

The technological leadership issue is, however, something entirely different. Such positions always assure the customer of the availability of the latest technology – and that's something that many customers want. Insofar our technological leadership is clearly linked to the CCA position."

The Disillusionment

Mr. Grey took the floor: "We are, after, all a technology-driven engineering company. Technological leadership is the expression of our marked innovative behaviour. When it comes to new technologies, we are nearly always the first past the post." "But technological leadership is only the basis for a potential CCA", Mark Etting interjected. "If we don't just want to discover, in other words make inventions, but make them commercially viable as well, so that customers can gain an additional benefit from them, then our invention orientation must be complemented by an innovation orientation including a successful market launch."

Birgit B. Blue leaned over to her colleague, Manni Meyer, and tapped him on the shoulder. "Mr. Meyer", she said to him quietly, "we're starting to go round in circles. We began the whole thing with 100 percent customer orientation and now we've got back to where we started. Is that how you see it too?" Manni Meyer, who was talking to a colleague from Production, turned round and replied: "I do Mrs. Blue. That's why I'm going to make a suggestion." He turned to face the whole auditorium, also catching the attention of Mark Etting in the process. "Dear colleagues, before we talk the entire matter to pieces, I would like to suggest that we simply try it out. Mr. Etting, send your people into the ranks and we'll proclaim 'the year of marketing'. This should give us something close to a one-year test market, and our orientation can then be re-discussed based on this experience." The workshop attendees all began to talk at once. In spite of the cacophony it was

possible to hear that the proposal had obviously se-
cured a majority vote. And Dick Discount mumbled to
himself with some relief: "Doubtless we'll get through
this year as well. Ideas come and ideas go, you simply
have to submerge yourself and let the waves wash
over you. It'll be just the same as last year when 'the
year of inventory reductions' was proclaimed. You
look to see how you can best get through the year
without sustaining too much damage. Improvements
are always possible. Afterwards everything goes back
to how it was before anyway." Manni Meyer was con-
vinced that proclaiming "the year of marketing" had
heralded the funeral process for the new marketing
ideas. He had thought that the company would develop from a company with a purely technological
orientation into a company with a more marked market orientation. But in his view that could not be
achieved by proclaiming "the year of marketing". Either they were ready to grasp the whole matter as a
fundamental and permanent phenomenon or they
would fail miserably. Market-oriented corporate management is a fundamental corporate decision that cannot be limited to one year.

Since people had got accustomed to longstanding
existing processes, he felt that this development had
come at just the right time. But Mark Etting's assess-
ment was a different one. He not only feared for his
standing but it had become blatantly clear to him that
in order to move forward he must now achieve a
breakthrough or, together with his marketing depart-

ment, drift slowly into insignificance. On the other hand, he was certain that he would no longer succeed in doing that in this particular workshop. For time was already running out and the participants were slowly losing patience.

The year of marketing appeared to be something that he recognized from politics. You achieve consensus on a secondary battlefield and sell this as the success of the negotiations. And he also knew that he could now say goodbye to the planned follow-up seminars that were intended to win over the broad majority of the workforce in favour of the company's new orientation. If the bosses were not sold on the idea of a market-oriented corporate management, and subsequently live it out in practice, then that which a staff member from the procurement department had told him in a previous seminar, would inevitably repeat itself time and again. He had said to him: "And when I then go home, my boss says to me: Well, did the seminar give you a chance to relax and recuperate? No doubt you've learned a great deal that we can all benefit from. Even so, it's good to have you back with us again. I'd like you to take care of our new project in Italy. We've already booked you on the first flight leaving for Milan tomorrow." All the new ideas that he had learned at the seminar and found interesting had been completely stripped away. He had been re-integrated as a cog in the wheels of the giant corporate machine almost instantly.

The Disillusionment

Mark Etting wanted to avoid this at all costs. It was clear to him that within the framework of his project he now found himself at a crucial stage. Yet the whole matter had started off with such promise, but now for some inexplicable reason it had reached an impasse. Nevertheless, he knew that he must now bring the workshop to a close in order to gain some time. He urgently needed to think of something to prevent 'the year of marketing' being proclaimed. For it was absolutely clear to him that if this were to happen, it would put pay to his entire strategy. What he needed was a good fairy to help him unearth the treasure of stringent market orientation slumbering deep within the company.

After having come so close to exposing this treasure chest, a thick layer of clay had covered it over again during the excavation process. "Why is it still the case that people only ever think about why something doesn't function properly instead of thinking about what needs to be done to implement a new concept successfully?" But that seemed to be a phenomenon that played a role in every organization It reminded him of his student days when he had learned from Professor Kotler that changes within a company – irrespective of what kind – faced three obstacles that needed to be overcome:

– organized resistance,

– slow learning,

– fast forgetting.

The Disillusionment

At DMA, Mark Etting had now found out just what that meant in concrete terms: Above all frustration! He was very close to giving up.

What had become of the enlightenment? Why are so many difficulties arising here? It's clear to everyone that something must happen. But it's not clear to anyone what that should be. We have established that from the perspective of those with functional responsibilities working out consistent proposals for a CCA is by no means easy. The reason for this lies on the one hand with the functional fixity of their thinking, i.e. in a selective perception of the overall process, and on the other also with the "beauty contest" mentality of the respective areas of responsibility that immunize themselves against criticism and change. Changes yes indeed, but not with me!

Mark Etting really does have a difficult task ahead of him. Let's see how he gets on.

Third Part
The Breakthrough

The Breakthrough

The meeting was not yet over. During a coffee break Mark Etting therefore approached Ernie Grey and expressed his doubts to him. But Ernie Grey was not about to entertain any negative thoughts or mood of depression. "We'll approach the process of change with a positive attitude and plenty of verve, Mark. We must win over our colleagues and the workforce because we really cannot carry on as before. I still find your ideas convincing. You shouldn't allow yourself to be so easily discouraged. Nevertheless, we must insist that everything we recommend should be measurable – just like it is on the cost side –, even though, admittedly, this is far more difficult for the revenue side."

Mark Etting was to explore such a concept with his team. If the results were up to his expectations, Ernie Grey would ensure that the package would be pushed seamlessly through. They couldn't carry on as they had been doing, that was pretty clear, and if they failed to make progress with the processes of change, then the crisis situation that was currently fertile for change, would develop into a situation that could endanger the company's entire stability. And that's something Ernie Grey wanted to avoid at all costs by taking corrective action promptly.

The discussion seemed to have run out of steam, so Ernie Grey used the remaining time to summarize the results and assign the tasks for the follow-up session taking place in 4 weeks time.

It was clear to Mark Etting that over these four weeks he would have to get a fundamental concept up and running. He was also very much aware that this process of change could turn into a Sisyphean task. Mark remembered Professor Kotler's three obstacles: organized resistance, slow learning and fast forgetting. But he also knew that Ernie Grey had now been fired with enthusiasm and if this were so – and many other cases proved it –, then he would bite into it like a terrier and not let go. That was just what Mark Etting needed at this moment in time.

On returning to his department, Mark Etting went over a number of things in his head. He resolved that once at home and in a more relaxed atmosphere he would try that very evening to organize his various thoughts and give them some kind of order. If he wanted to permanently anchor market orientation as a corporate policy and corporate behaviour/practice, he needed to have a clear structure in front of him. What he didn't want was for market orientation to degenerate into a fashion trend that could then be superseded by other fashion trends. That evening was predestined for such a task: His live-in girlfriend had taken herself off to a wellness hotel for three days with her Bodyfit Group to get a chance to relax and chill out. Thus Mark Etting was able to concentrate fully on the matter in hand and didn't have to listen to anybody constantly reminding him that although he was home, he was in fact elsewhere. So as not to be disturbed or once again be accused of turning the kitchen into a slaughter house in his girlfriend's absence, today on the way home he intended stopping off at a fast-food restaurant to order a take-away of two hamburgers with a double portion of French fries.

Mark Etting had left the office as early as 5:00 p.m. in order to be able to devote as much of the evening as possible to his deliberations. By 6:00 p.m. he was already sitting in front of his two hamburgers with the French fries smothered in mayonnaise and ketchup which he consumed without uttering a word. He then set about applying himself to the subject-matter of how best to create a market-oriented corporate management.

First of all he wanted to change the planning. The planning of the CCA should be the central element within the framework of corporate planning. As he had previously emphasized, it seemed to him that DMA's planning was too deeply rooted in statistics. The planning of the CCA would highlight the importance of the navigator in DMA's entire planning system. Any scheduled market share changes and sales forecasts ought to be backed up and justified by a CCA analysis. If he could convince Ernie Grey that this was a "conditio sine qua non", then he would be out of the woods. With it he would not be restricted to just preaching the CCA concept in seminars, but the hard facts would save him from having to apply the missionary touch.

Secondly, he would ensure that all the departments in the company defined what contribution they make towards achieving a jointly defined CCA position. Those departments being unable to envisage making a

CCA contribution should be subjected to a special analysis. Because in Mark Etting's view it simply didn't make any sense to maintain departments – unless legally required – that don't provide any added value to customers and thus don't make any contribution towards generating revenue. That would divest the discussion about the CCA also of its purely seminar character and integrate it into the actual operational planning process. After the debacle in the CCA workshop that was particularly important to him.

Finally, it was also very much clear to him that he would have to create an incentive scheme to reward market orientation. However, that was not quite so easy because in terms of marketing the various products required different key indicators. For instance, there was a section in the company referred to as the solutions business that implemented individualized turn-key projects while in other department standard machines with a much lower demand for customization were sold. While in the solution business the price did not play such a marked role, the standard machine business had grown into a business that was based virtually on price alone. Unless Mark Etting wanted to fail as a result of the practical needs of the executive departments, these differences had to be taken into account in the marketing-related key indicators. Developing such a comprehensive system would take some time but certainly meet Ernie Grey's expectations most precisely.

The Breakthrough

Ernie Grey would surely accept the additional time necessary if Mark were able to present him with a timetable that contained concrete milestones. Mark therefore keyed a reminder into his smartphone: "Discuss, brainstorm and develop market orientation key indicator system with staff members of the departments." He noted a two-month period for completing this. But he also knew that this alone would not be enough by any means to help a market orientation perspective, capable of living up to this name, experience a breakthrough. That's why he wanted to have the concept completely finished first before attempting a fresh start.

Two weeks later the results of the round of talks were at hand. The participants had retreated for a whole week to the Palace Hotel Bilfingen, whereby Mark Etting had placed a complete ban on the use of mobiles. He allowed the participants a 15-minute "mobile slot" just twice a day, during which time they had the chance to get rid of their "communication clutter".

The outcome was impressive. Firstly, over several days the participants developed a concentrated weakness analysis which set up as it were warning signs indicating what mistakes needed to be avoided in implementing a consistent market orientation. Marketing representatives from associated companies had also been invited at short notice who reported, sometimes in detail, about their corresponding setbacks and frustrating experiences. Emerging as key warning signs were above all the following issues:

The absence of a systematic customer analysis

The emphasis placed here was on systematic customer analysis. What applied to many companies also applied to DMA: the respective sales engineers had their customers in their heads and knew a surprising number of details. Unfortunately, this knowledge wasn't systematically recorded, so every time a sales engineer left the company it was irretrievably lost and had to be built up again. It was clear to Mark Etting that only a CRM system (Customer Relation Management System) could ultimately help here which – supported by an EDP system – would make any compilation of information from the collated customer data possible. However, everyone making up the group of marketing specialists was in agreement that the term CRM systems should initially be withheld. The entire matter was otherwise at risk of degenerating into an IT problem, in other words would be met with resistance from the sales force. Previous rounds of talks had already made that pretty clear. But Mark Etting was very much aware that in the long run this issue would have to be addressed. A staff questionnaire issued some time ago enquiring as to what one associates with the term „research", had clearly shown that research has apparently nothing to do with market research, at least as perceived by the workforce. Whenever the term „research" was mentioned, it always involved technological or scientific research. It was obvious that market research was not included in the range of research topics.

Lack of honest admittance that CCAs are in short supply

"When the employees are requested to define their CCAs, then there is practically no-one who is able to come up with at least something. In this regard we can differentiate between two types of employees. The first type of employee has a clear idea of what the CCA is, on the basis of which his/her value chain sells. The participant involved in making the observation referred to the second group as 'the slightly better approach'. This approach was characterized by a number of CCA dimensions being given as part of the CCA. Nevertheless, in the eyes of the consumer the supplier here was always only marginally better, thus running the risk of the customer not perceiving it as a difference. What was often lacking was the focus on a few but clear CCA dimensions. One of the invited guests quoted an example, by way of which he made clear what it means to focus on just a few CCA dimensions, but to use them to generate clear perception advantages over the offers of competitors." Doris Guestspeaker, one of the invited marketing employees of an associated company, demonstrated this by citing an example: "In my company I have found it extremely difficult to get people to focus on a central CCA message. You will know that we are manufacturers of harvesting machines and have spent a great deal of time considering what kind of situation represents the worst-case scenario for a farmer. You will also be aware that nearly all the harvesting machines we sell are not bought by an individual farmer but by farmers in farmers' cooperatives who then share the use of the harvesting machine. The sad thing about the whole affair is that all the farmers want to use the harvesting machine at the very same time because the harvest doesn't take place for different farmers at different times. That's why the cooperatives keep lists recording which farmer has access to the harvesting machine and at what time. During harvest time the harvesting machines are therefore operated day and night. They are deployed for 24 hours around the clock. In these circumstances the worst-case scenario for a farmer is, for example, when at 4 o' clock in the morning he gets stuck in furrow number 17 because the harvesting machine has a defect but must still hand it over to the neighbouring farmer at 7 o'clock that morning. That's why we have developed a system in our company, whereby the farmer finds a large sticker on his harvesting machine recommending that in the case of a defect occurring day or night he should ring a special number. A call to this number initiates a specific process within our company. Firstly, as soon as the farmer makes the call his identification code, emitted via the telephone number, is immediately registered and the staff working in shifts around the clock automatically get a message on the screen indicating what type of harvesting machine is involved. A checklist is then produced, with the aid of which the member of staff manning the phone confronts the farmer in trouble.

His answers lead to an automatically generated prognosis as to what the problem could be. This member of staff informs the house mechanic saying: 'Hermann, for you the night is over, the harvesting machine no. 323/012 is stuck in furrow 17. It's probably the following problem, so take this or the other spare part with you.'

The mechanic heads for the farmer and is more than likely able to rectify the problem or repair the damage quickly on site.

We log all these incidents in a database which we evaluate at regular intervals. As more and more incidents are recorded, we get increasingly better at diagnosing what the problems could be. We have since progressed to such an extent that no matter where a farmer is in Germany we can give a 'get-it-fixed 4-hour guarantee' which we even attach a penalty to. The customer sees this as an exceptionally favourable use benefit and is willing to also pay corresponding price surcharges for this guarantee. You can therefore see that our CCA lies not so much in the hardware but rather in a cleverly organized service that incorporates a significant price potential. What's more this CCA is not easy to imitate because based on our experience of the malfunction/damage symptoms we know what the problem with the harvesting machine could potentially be. A competitor cannot quickly imitate this CCA because the expert knowledge necessary must first be built up over a longer period of time. Our communication policy and personal selling focuses entirely on this service advantage and, as you know, we are extremely successful with it." "An excellent example" Mark Etting commented. "Perhaps we should develop something similar for our own machines, but that's a decision for the departments with line functions."

Product advantage or use benefit?

That a CCA can also comprise clearly verifiable service benefits has been demonstrated by the previous example. "Our people still think too much in terms of product benefits rather than in terms of perceived CCAs", one of Mark Etting's team members remarked. "This is to do with the fact that we operate a business dominated by technology. The fully automated mouse trap with automatic disposal may well have a host of product benefits but does the customer really need all that? Perhaps he needs to see the proof of a dead mouse or is simply overwhelmed by the automation because he is required to reprogramme the mouse trap every time. You must always bear in mind that a product advantage only leads to a CCA when it also generates a use benefit. The example of the harvesting machine demonstrates this perfectly. Engineers and technicians often don't see that a product advantage does not necessarily constitute a perceived use benefit." "I don't know how you feel about it" Doris Guestspeaker had said in the Palace Hotel Bilfingen, "but the new TVs offer fantastic save and store options. These are real product advantages. If someone rings the door bell when you're watching an exciting film, you can get the

TV to record the missing sequence so that you can continue watching the film in time-shift mode at the exact point where you left off. The only problem is that I don't know how to operate this technical procedure, meaning that a major product advantage is not turned into a perceived use benefit. I've still got my old video recording system, which admittedly doesn't offer me time-shift mode, but I'm able to operate it perfectly Even so, the same applies here also: every two weeks I have to record a film, not necessarily because I want to add it to my video collection but simply because I don't want to forget how the recording process works." This produced lively laughter at the Palace Hotel Bilfingen because in this statement many of those present had obviously recognized their own problems.

Inadequate knowledge about the competition

You cannot define a CCA properly because the relevant knowledge about your competitors is often unavailable. "Our Competitive Intelligence Department collects every piece of information about our competitors that you can get hold of. In specific circumstances, however, it frequently doesn't prove of any benefit because the information relevant for a decision is often missing. I would like to make this clear by citing an example", Triple B said. "As you know, we manufacture, among other things, small standard machines for simple turning operations. That's exclusively a commodity business. As you perhaps know better than myself, with commodities price plays a central role. Already during my student days I learned that successful price leader positions require cost leader positions, if you don't just want to produce losses long term. Our Competitive Intelligence Department had collected together all the relevant information about the competitors we would face on entering the market in this standard machines segment. However, we were missing a central piece of information, namely what experience curves are relevant for which competitors.

Our CI Department was not in a position to obtain this information in a timely fashion. One of my colleagues set about finding out whether the relevant competitors – a total of five competitors were involved – all produce themselves and thus had their own experience curves or whether they perhaps purchased their products from one or several suppliers, which products they would then individualize through corresponding branding activities. To our great surprise we found that all our competitors purchased goods from one Taiwanese manufacturer, so it was clear to us that our main opponent – with regard to the cost leader position – must be the Taiwanese supplier. As far as the relevant information is concerned, our CI Department had practically no knowledge about our competitors."

Slow learning processes

"CCAs should have a certain durability in order for marketing strategies to be built up around them",

Mark Etting summed up with reference to a further weakness in the implementation of marketing ideas. "But as a rule they don't last forever. And the problem is, the bigger the CCA, the safer you feel. The day-to-day business simply covers everything up. We must realize, however, that we live in markets that have high competitive dynamics. We have to adapt in good time. In reality, however, adapting to the competitive dynamics takes place too late and takes too long."

„The reason for this", one of the guests interjected, "is that most companies don't have a continuous flow of information and communication through the entire value chain. Sales frequently doesn't know what R&D is doing and vice versa. Everyone lives and thinks in their own department. I like to refer to it as the archipelago syndrome. Everyone participating in a value chain tries to create their own island, on which they can live happily. But it is absolutely essential not to think in terms of the department but in terms of the added value." "We have to make people understand this", one of Mark Etting's team summarized.

A lack of creativity and vision

"One central weakness in our company" said one of the guests, "was the fact that we had begun to herald in our market orientation by starting a whole series of seminars. After one week we had made sufficient progress, I believe, that our people basically understood what marketing was all about. Following these seminar sessions I received a host of calls asking for checklists showing how market orientation could be implemented. It's similar to a pilot starting a plane and checking that he hasn't forgotten anything and that everything is correctly set. But market orientation cannot be generated in this way. Market orientation requires creativity and vision and cannot be managed by filling out and working through a checklist. We need broad, open and unbiased thinking that allows issues to be observed, also from a competition-relevant perspective. In the process, even absolutely small measures can have a relatively major impact.

I'm not above citing you an old anecdote that puts the relativity issue into a nutshell. Two trappers are out and about in the Canadian forests to hunt bears. One evening while sitting around the camp fire roasting chicken legs, one of the trappers suddenly turns to the other and says: 'There's a bear behind you.' The second trapper turns round very, very slowly to find a grizzly bear stood on its hind legs towering over him.

He calmly puts down the chicken leg he was eating, stands up and disappears into his tent. After two minutes he reappears wearing a pair of old trainers on his feet. The first trapper says: 'What's all that about? The shoes won't help you. The bear is quicker than you with or without trainers.' The trapper wearing the trainers replies: 'You obviously don't know what a CCA is. I don't have to be faster than the bear, just faster than you.'

Or think back to our example of the harvesting machines where it was a matter of finding a clearly communicable CCA that couldn't have been found in any checklist. Market orientation therefore demands creativity. Without being able to think of anything that is of benefit to the customer, better still that is more beneficial than competing products, it just won't work. But creativity cannot be generated by checklists. If you can't think of anything creative that distinguishes you from the competition, then don't expect the customer to come up with something either."

Against the backdrop of these considerations the team around Mark Etting had designed a process, with which in the view of the marketing department the change management from a technology orientation to an increased market orientation could be successful. The core of the concept and its launch for the market orientation of DMA was to be a renewed dialogue with the management. What Mark Etting hoped to achieve in this dialogue was to get the entire management to commit itself to this subject-matter. The marketing success key figures concept that had since been developed was also to be approved. The management would have to make clear that they would monitor and control its realization. Over and above this the CCA was to become a central element in DMA's planning system. Ultimately, the result of successful customer orientation was also to become measurable in statistics. And in conclusion the company was to be reorganized because the existing organizational structures had already become too deep-rooted and were not market-oriented. The orientation framework for the new organization was to be the customer-focussed organization of value chains. With it Mark Etting wanted to implement customer orientation organizationally and sustainably within the company – namely in the frontline. Mark Etting was well aware that only if the management were prepared to go along with this process and support it, would they have a chance of breaking with the company's old mould of thinking. At the same time he also knew that if he failed to convince the management to approve this concept, greater market orientation would never be possible. Then the same old story would happily repeat itself, i.e. the realization of cost-cutting programmes to improve results.

In case this should actually happen, Mark Etting had prepared a short text that he had extracted from Oswald Neuberger's book "Was ist denn da so komisch?" (*"What's so funny then?"*), with a few small changes of his own.

It involved a fictitious report about an action plan devised by the company McKinsey for the Berlin Philharmonic Orchestra.

"The four oboists hadn't had anything to do for quite a while. The number was to be shortened and the work spread evenly across the entire orchestra to avoid peak workloads. The twelve violinists all play the same. That's an unnecessary duplication of effort. This group was to be drastically downsized. If a higher volume is desired, this can be achieved using an electronic sound system.

The playing of demisemiquavers requires a huge amount of effort. It is recommended that these notes be combined with the nearest semiquavers. It would then be possible to also employ music students and less qualified musicians.

In a number of parts there are too many repetitions. As a result, the scores are to be completely reworked. It serves no useful purpose if the horn repeats a passage that the violins have already played. If all the superfluous passages are eliminated, then the concert that now last two hours, is estimated to last no longer than twenty minutes, meaning that the usual break midway through can be dispensed with.

The conductor doesn't dispute the fact that this recommendation is justified but fears there will be a fall in box office takings as a result. In this unlikely event it ought then be possible to close parts of the concert hall entirely which would allow costs to be saved for light, staff etc. If the worst should come to the worst the concert hall itself could be closed and the people sent to the concert coffee house. ... "

Mark Etting laughed aloud. A wonderful report about a pointless cost-cutting measure that is so wonderfully over-exaggerated that it illustrates perfectly where an orientation based solely on costs can lead to. Although a number of responses from others were still outstanding, Ernie Grey got to his feet and ended the discussion.

"Ladies and gentlemen, we have discussed long enough and heard some interesting examples from other companies. So now we know what is important when it comes to a CCA and we are all agreed that with the CCA we have found the right compass for a market-oriented strategy that really deserves this name. I now expect from every value chain concrete proposals that we can work further with!" Ernie Grey sensed something like a renewed spirit of optimism which he immediately exploited to get the leaders of the various value chains to commit to the new strategy. "Gentlemen, I expect from you that we briefly collate what concepts we can spontaneously think of."

This statement brought forth wild responses from the participants. Ernie Grey first allowed Benny Miller, Head of the Standard Machines Division, to take the floor. "What we operate is a purely commodity-based business which – as we all know – is a distinctly price-driven business. However, we have too little volume to be able to realize a true CCA based on price because our cost position doesn't allow it. I suggest that we define our CCA with a new pricing policy. A few weeks ago I was talking to a Telecom employee who explained to me how the telecommunications branch imposes differential pricing on the market for the commodity 'phone call'. They call it 'non-linear pricing (NLP)'. This NLP concept could also form the basis of an interesting CCA position for us. One form of NLP involves multi-component pricing whereby the price comprises several components, e.g. a basic charge and a variable charge. This would be a revolutionary pricing policy for our standard machines – along the lines of the motto: We reduce the sales price of the machine by half and the customer pays a charge for every turned part."

Benny Miller's deliberations led to such vehement comments from the participants that the discussion was in danger of completely falling apart. "Enough, enough", Ernie Grey called out. "It appears that I have now made clear what all this is about. That's enough for today. Mark Etting will send one member of his staff to every division to assist the managing director in properly formulating the CCA positions. We will meet again in four weeks and I will go through every single suggestion with you together with Mark. In any event we will have approved the entire strategy before the summer break."

In the weeks that followed the marketing department was assigned the task of coordinating the newly developed lines of communication between the various "departmental islands". For the very first time the developers conversed with people from Production and with the sales engineers. They all got to know entirely new worlds. R&D learned to recognize production problems early on and to already take these into account at the development stage.

Quality Assurance learned that quality may mean the 100 percent fulfilment of customers' wishes but that the customers' wishes vary from segment to segment, and the members of the sales team set themselves the task of making their customer knowledge accessible to everyone involved. The figures for sales and earnings rose again significantly and even exceeded all expectations.

How did it come about that the breakthrough finally succeeded? The first and key success factor can be attributed to the management making it their central task to demand and enforce market orientation time and again, and thus understand and implement marketing as a true leadership task. This in turn allows a marketing culture to establish itself because the management has understood that the management of CCAs is a never-ending process that constantly calls for new input.

We thus see that if we want to facilitate the breakthrough of a lived market orientation, it has to be clear that the management must make it their task to overcome by personal commitment the disillusionment phase that always occurs. This includes the control and monitoring of the marketing measures as well. In his function as Head of Marketing Mark Etting can then assume the role he is entitled to, namely to coordinate the company's market presence in order to successfully devise a way out of the crisis and make the company successful again.

It is important, though, to defend even in "good times" that which was achieved to overcome this crisis. To proclaim "the year of marketing" is therefore counterproductive. Market orientation must be enforced time and again. It is an ongoing process, or as Mark Etting has formulated it: a Sisyphean task.

Epilogue

Marketing and its position at the board table

Thus, in this particular instance – as in most other cases too – the realization of market orientation is not so much an external problem but more of an internal problem. This applies in particular to the marketing of industrial goods. The alignment of all members of a value chain to a specific CCA or several CCAs contradicts the conventional thinking of many employees within a company. They have learned to think in functional islands. These islands have their own specific departmental culture. That's why it is also a corporate-cultural challenge to consistently align oneself to the market and the customers. At the same time it becomes clear that customer and market orientation is not an end in itself but a means to an end. This means making a profit – and customer/ market orientation is a way to achieve this. The goal here is not to fulfil the customers' wishes 100 percent – as many advisors call for, but rather to realize a perceived higher level of fulfilment of the customers' wishes compared with all other competitors operating in the market. This value can be significantly lower than 100 percent. We therefore reiterate: marketing belongs at the board table. If that isn't clear, each form of marketing will degenerate into a purely instrumental consideration. For such an instrumental interpretation it is sufficient to explore both market and customer and with it place the external perspective at the centre of all activities. The story of DMA has, however, shown that the internal perspective is perhaps the more important one: it's a matter of making it clear to everyone working in the company that market orientation is really desired. And this is a non-delegable managerial responsibility. If you're serious about marketing, then you have to anchor it at the board table.